# Paper Cranes and The Things We Lost Along The Way

Luke Halliday

BookLeaf Publishing

Presentation by *BookLeaf Publishing*

Web: www.bookleafpub.com

E-mail: info@bookleafpub.com

ISBN: 978-93-95755-31-3

First edition 2022

*For my Nan, to put on her bookshelf.*

# Life is but a dream

A letter I wrote, from some time back,
Spoke of my memories, now turned black,
How could I forget, those brilliant times,
When being free, was our only crime,
Making paper cranes from serviettes,
Laughing, crying and feeling regret,
Running around, hoping to take flight,
To become a star, lighting the night,
How do I know, those times were real,
When they are too far, for me to feel?
Back then, everything was as it seemed,
But now it appears; life is but a dream.

# In My Own Words

There is a lonesome sound
Of the boy I used to be.
Freedom in the lost and found,
Which of you, is the real me?
Falling apart seems so easy
When you've never been whole.
Lying in the space that's in between
Your restless heart and fragile soul.
That lonely boy I used to be,
The man I am, lost at sea.
Speaking a language in tongue and cheek.
I just want to love you in my own words.

# Answers in Alaska

Like a puzzle piece that just doesn't fit,
Open your eyes and see that this is it,
You're getting more tired as days go by,
You find eternities in the back of your mind,
Lonesome blues run through your head,
you can't make the dead not dead,
So many things you have left to say,
Maybe Bruce was right, they'll come back some day?
So drop the needle and take a spin around Alaska,
Maybe you'll find the lost answers you've been after?

# Bronte

I was 19 standing by the beach at Bronte, I
thought it'd be okay to die out there.
I'd swim out far, chasing stars and be swallowed
by the sea. For all I'd done, that would be fair.
It's been a while since I felt that way, I promise
you, I swear.
But if I told you that all the lights in the sky
were stars would you think of me up there?
A note left online, I try to hit delete, it wasn't
me, I was hacked I'd bet.  It was all damn regret,
so can you take those things I said and just
forget?

# Embers Of You

My memories unfold a story told a thousand
years ago,
This may be the furthest I've ever been, from
you.
Yet I am here living with your ghost.
 The delicate details organize themselves in my
mind behind my eyes,
The image you like the planets in retrograde
each hidden by the moon,
 A touch of your grace,
A waking dream tender and sweet,
Lost in an instant behind the waves that crash
against me and take me deep below.
 Now I know how the stars appear from the
bottom of the sea,
Embers of you among the blue.

# The Sway

Out of rhythm, though we got that sway,
Under these city lights, we dance the same way,
Unspoken words, our fleeting hearts race,
Speaking in motion, our souls embrace,
Explosions in the sky, the song comes to an end,
A bittersweet goodbye, pray we dance again.

# The Same Flame

A smouldering sunset
Her burning embrace
As July meets November
These things we remember
The miracle that we met
The look upon her face
A new kind of love
Lit by the same flame

# November

All that remains are smokey memories,
Up so high looking out to sea,
Late night drives, no place to be,
Sitting in our park, just us three,
When you broke my heart, she cried for me,
Your lie in November, no love comes free,
Playing pretend, like it's all a bad dream,
Feeling lucid, now I know what it means,
This is how to disappear completely.

# Quiet Tonight

It's quiet tonight
Here without you two
Only the sound of thunder
Rolling through my room
And the smell of smoke
On my body like a tattoo
Yeah, it's quiet tonight
Do you feel it too?

# Never Knows Best

Smoke burns out between her lips,
I guess you'll never know if you always miss,
Let it all slip away through your fingertips,
Never knows best when you let life slip,
What will be the soundtrack of your life?
A sound to a scene, you play it back in your
mind,
Let the feeling hit you like a meteorite,
Never knows best when you only hit rewind.

# The Blues

Feeling alone in a crowded room.
Even though you know somebody loves you.
Feeling lost and feeling confused.
Never knowing where you're going or what
you're gonna do.
Following your heart like you've got nothing to
lose.
Just dancing in the dark and singing the blues.

# This Hurt

I'm not really scared of dying,
Sometimes I'm just scared of living,
I tell you I'm okay,
But who am I kidding?
You or me? I don't even know.
They say the first step is admitting.
To be erased or to become a ghost,
If I disappeared, would you know I was
missing?
She tells me others have it so much worse,
But that doesn't change that I'm still this hurt.
Please don't speak, don't say a word.
I just need to vent and to be heard.
No, I'm not scared of the fire.
I know how it feels to be burned.
I'm just scared of desire
And this pain that I've learned.

# Not Today

All these things that we've done,  Erased,
swallowed by the sea. Goodbyes are hard, it's
easier to run, Did you forget to remember me?
Who can I be now? Solitary swaying, I lost
myself somewhere on the way here,
I can still hear that Fleetwood song playing
And those words you whispered in my ear,
You'll be okay.
Just not today.

# This Digital Dream

I figured by now I'd have figured things out.
That I'd understand the meaning and what life's
all about.
But I'm still as lost as eighteen at twenty eight.
I never really learned how to live in a way I can
relate.
Am I too honest and say things better kept
inside?
I make a mess of things almost every single
time.
Things would be easier if people said what they
mean.
But they're all too busy living this digital dream.

# Ashes to Ashes

The embers of you still burn in me,
Like a fire inside of my memory,
Ashes to ashes of a life that's been,
I wish I could still tell you what you meant to
me,
Now that I know who I'm supposed to be.

# Digital Separation

The final chords rang out
and the song was over
I thought we had more time
now there is only distance between us
and feint sounds heard years ago
of a time when I was easier to love
and heartbreak felt so shiny and new
now I just read about the things that you do
through the cold embrace of digital separation

# One Click Away

Feeling so reachable, so accessible, just one
click away.
I want to disappear, go offline and be okay.
We're all so damn connected but I just want an
escape.

# Scheherazade

Every time I close my eyes,
I'm dreaming of Scheherazade.
Countless days and countless nights,
It's always, my Scheherazade.

# Birdland

Too many goodbyes and words left unsaid.
I'll never be the boy I was again.
I can still hear them playing Lullaby of Birdland.

# Wishes

Did Sadako ever finish folding her paper cranes? I guess there are some wishes we just take to the grave.

# It's Okay

Growing old but still getting young,
Tried to write it down, it's all be done,
Better say something a little less dumb,
But talking academic just ain't no fun,
It's hard to breathe when you're with the one,
Heart stops beating when you got that some,
Who says that's not how it's supposed to be
done?
Can't find the words, maybe there are none,
Life's a crawl until you learn how to run,
Like George said, here comes that sun,
Are you satisfied with who you've become?
Are you okay with all you've done?
Did you lose yourself trying to be someone?
How do you undo what can't be undone?
Dreams come true but you feel so numb.
It's okay, the best days are still to come.

9 789395 755313